A Soldier's Life in the Civil War

Dale Anderson

WORLD ALMANAC® LIBRARY

Please visit our web site at: www.worldalmanaclibrary.com
For a free color catalog describing World Almanac® Library's
list of high-quality books and multimedia programs,
call 1-800-848-2928 (USA) or 1-800-387-3178 (Canada).
World Almanac® Library's fax: (414) 332-3567.

Library of Congress Cataloging-in-Publication Data available
upon request from publisher. Fax (414) 336-0157 for the
attention of the Publishing Records Department.

ISBN 0-8368-5586-8 (lib. bdg.)
ISBN 0-8368-5595-7 (softcover)

First published in 2004 by
World Almanac® Library
330 West Olive Street, Suite 100
Milwaukee, WI 53212 USA

Produced by Discovery Books
Project editor: Geoff Barker
Editor: Valerie J. Weber
Designer and page production: Laurie Shock, Shock Design, Inc.
Photo researcher: Rachel Tisdale
Consultant: Andrew Frank, Assistant Professor of History, Florida
    Atlantic University
Maps: Stefan Chabluk
World Almanac® editorial direction: Mark Sachner
World Almanac® art direction: Tammy Gruenewald

Photo credits: Corbis: cover, pp. 8, 11, 15, 16, 22 (top), 23, 24, 25, 27
(top), 28, 30, 33 (bottom), 34, 36, 40, 43; Peter Newark's American
Pictures: pp. 7, 9, 12, 14, 17, 19, 20 (both), 22 (bottom), 27 (bottom),
37, 39; Library of Congress: title page, pp. 2, 10, 18, 29, 33 (top); State
Archives of Michigan: p. 31; Museum of the Confederacy: p. 35;
Bettmann/CORBIS: p. 42.

Printed in the United States of America

1 2 3 4 5 6 7 8 9 08 07 06 05 04

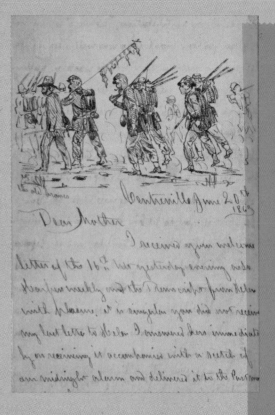

*"To my mother, who got me
Bruce Catton; my brother,
who shared my passion for the
Civil War; and my wife and
sons, who cheerfully put up
with several field trips and
countless anecdotes."*

— DALE ANDERSON

Cover: The clothes of these three Confederate soldiers,
taken prisoner after the Battle of Gettysburg in 1863,
reveal the lack of regular uniforms that was common
among Southern soldiers.

Contents

Confederate and Union States in 1861

While the Confederate states covered about as much territory as the Union states, they held fewer people, fewer factories, and fewer railroad tracks and locomotives. These would be significant drawbacks for the Confederacy during the Civil War. The South would also lose part of its support when West Virginia separated from the rest of Virginia in 1863.

The War between the States

The Civil War was fought between 1861 and 1865. It was the bloodiest conflict in United States history, with more soldiers killed and wounded than in any other war. It was also a pivotal event in U.S. history: It transformed the lives of millions of African-American men, women, and children by freeing them from slavery. It also transformed the nation, changing it from a loose confederation of states into a powerful country with a strong central government.

On one side were eleven southern states that had split from the United States to form a new country, the Confederate States of America, led by President Jefferson Davis. They took this step after Abraham Lincoln was elected president of the United

States in 1860. Southerners feared Lincoln would end slavery, which was central to their economy and society. The northern states, or the **Union**, declared this split illegal.

A big question was whether the four **Border States** (Delaware, Maryland, Kentucky, and Missouri) would join the **Confederacy**. They had slavery, too, but they also held many people loyal to the Union. To keep control of these states, Lincoln felt early in the war that he could not risk moving against slavery, fearing that to do so would drive the Border States out of the Union. Later, however, he did declare the emancipation, or freedom, of Southern slaves.

In the Border States, and in many others, families divided sharply, with some men fighting for one side and some for the other. The Civil War has been called a war of "brother against brother."

Fighting broke out on April 12, 1861, when gunners for the South began shelling Union soldiers in Fort Sumter in Charleston Harbor, South Carolina. This attack led Lincoln to call for troops to put down what he called an armed rebellion. Thousands of Northerners flocked to the Union army. Thousands of Southerners joined the Confederate army, determined to win independence for their side.

Soldiers in both the Union and Confederate armies suffered the hardships—and occasional boredom—of life in an army camp. They also fought in huge battles with great bravery and heroism. At times, both sides treated their enemies with honor and respect. At other times, they treated them with cruelty and brutality.

The opposing armies fought in two main areas, or theaters. The eastern theater included Pennsylvania, Virginia, and Maryland; the region near the Confederate capital of Richmond, Virginia; and the Union capital of Washington, D.C. The huge western theater stretched from eastern Kentucky and Tennessee down to the Gulf of Mexico and all the way to New Mexico. By the end of the many bloody battles across these lands, the Union won in 1865, and the states reunited into a single country.

Hundreds of thousands of men served in the armies and navies of the Union and the Confederacy during the Civil War. Almost all of them were volunteers—people who left their normal lives to join in the army. They found life in the army very different from what they had known as civilians.

CHAPTER ONE

Building the Armies

"Father, we must have more soldiers. This Union your ancestors and mine helped to make must be saved from destruction. I can better go than some others. I don't feel right to stay at home any longer."

Ted Upson, sixteen-year-old Union volunteer, 1861

~

A Call to Arms

As the war began in 1861, Confederate president Jefferson Davis and Union president Abraham Lincoln both needed to raise armies. On March 6, the Congress of the Confederacy—the law-making body of the South—gave Davis the power to raise an army of 100,000 volunteers for a year. In July 1861, the Congress of the Union called for up to one million volunteers to serve three years.

In January 1861, just after the Confederate states began to **secede**, the federal army contained about 16,400 men. Fewer than three hundred officers and over two dozen enlisted men resigned to join the Confederacy.

Early in the war, volunteers were eager to join the war effort. Southerners wanted to defend their homes and saw themselves as continuing the American Revolution by rebelling anew against a too-powerful central government. Northerners wanted to defend the Union created in that earlier war.

Whatever the cause, volunteers poured into both armies, encouraged by rallies that stirred up patriotic feelings. Some men wanted to impress a young woman or were pressured by wives or mothers. Many women, however, deeply

ATTENTION, TO SAVE YOUR BOUNTY!
SECOND REGIMENT
EMPIRE BRIGADE!
Col. P. J. CLAASSEN, Commanding.
FIRST REGIMENT IN THE FIELD UNDER THE NEW CALL.

WANTED, 25 MEN
Between the ages of 18 and 45 years, to fill up one of the best Companies now forming, under officers who have seen active service.
Clothing, Subsistence and Comfortable Quarters provided on enlistment.
PAY FROM $13 TO $23 PER MONTH,
TO DATE FROM DAY OF ENLISTMENT.
$50 BOUNTY GIVEN BY THE STATE.
$25 BOUNTY GIVEN BY THE U. S. GOVERNMENT.
TO BE PAID AS SOON AS MUSTERED INTO SERVICE.
$100 BOUNTY WHEN THE WAR IS OVER!
It is intended to make this one of the best Companies in the Brigade or service and no labor will be spared to do so. The Officers are experienced men, having been over one year in one of the First Regiments in the service.
CAPTAIN J. H. STINER, LATE OF HAWKINS ZOUAVES.

BAKER & GODWIN, Printers, Printing-House Square, opposite City Hall, N. Y.

Recruiting posters like these were the television commercials of the time, using calls to patriotism—and offers of money such as the $50 bounty paid by the state and the $25 bounty paid by the Union government—to persuade men to volunteer.

feared what might happen to their husbands and sons in the war.

The Organization of Units

The chief organizational unit was the **regiment**. Union regiments held about one thousand soldiers, but Confederate ones were smaller.

Regiments carried the name of the state where they were organized, producing names like the First Mississippi or the Seventy-eighth Pennsylvania. Some had colorful nicknames, such as the Louisiana Tigers, the Palmetto Guard of South Carolina, the Chicago Light Dragoons, or New York's Garibaldi Guards. Often one or more of the ten companies in a regiment—and sometimes the entire regiment—came from a single town or city. This was disastrous for that locality, of course, when the regiment suffered heavy **casualties**.

The way regiments were organized hurt effectiveness. Casualties and illness cut into each regiment's strength. The wise course would have been to send new recruits to replace these troops, which would give the newcomers a chance to learn from veterans. State governors on both sides, however, preferred to form completely new units so they could point with pride to the number of units they sent to the war. This also gave them more chances to reward friends by naming them officers in a regiment.

Composed of soldiers trained and equipped to fight on foot, infantry units were organized into larger groupings. Three to six regiments made a brigade. Two to six

FLAGS

Regiments carried special flags that indicated the regiment's name and the battles it had fought in. The flag bearer moved the flag in different ways to pass on the regimental commander's orders to advance, regroup, or retreat to the troops. Regimental colors also served as a point of pride to the unit's officers and men. For both reasons, flag bearers were often the targets of enemy fire. A captured regimental flag was a highly valued prize in battle.

Along with a regimental flag, Union regiments carried a national flag. This one, belonging to the Eighth Pennsylvania, saw fierce fighting.

brigades were combined into divisions, and two to four divisions were joined to make a corps, which consisted of 20,000 to 30,000 soldiers. At first, there was no way of distinguishing between any of these units. Over time, the Union armies came to use distinctive badges for each corps—a cross, triangle, star, or other symbol. The Confederate armies did not adopt such a system.

The Later Need for Soldiers

As the war dragged on, both sides needed to add to their armies. Enthusiasm waned, however, and it became more difficult to find new recruits. Some soldiers also wrote letters home to friends and family, urging them not to join. War and fighting, they said, was not all glorious. In the North, the economy was booming and wages were rising; people would rather work than risk their lives in war.

Southern Solutions

The recruiting problem hit first in the South because most of its first volunteers had only signed up for one year, and by 1862, their terms of enlistment were running out. The South responded by creating a **draft**. Males between eighteen and thirty-five were

In March 1864, a crowd gathers outside a New York City army recruiting station full of signs detailing the cash rewards that men could collect if they joined the army.

required to join the army for three years, though there were exceptions for people in some key jobs, such as doctors and teachers. Later laws extended these ages down to seventeen and up to fifty.

A later law also gave exemptions to men who owned twenty or more slaves—which only the wealthiest Southerners, such as plantation owners, could afford. Many Southerners protested that this exemption made the war "a rich man's war and a poor man's fight." Adding to these complaints was the fact that men could hire another as a substitute, some-

thing again that only the rich could afford to do.

Fewer than 100,000 men were drafted into the Confederate army, partially because of exemptions and the hiring of substitute soldiers. Several state governors also resisted the draft law since they thought it gave too much power to the central government and violated the rights of the states. On the other hand, the draft law did spur volunteering since volunteers were allowed to create new regiments and choose their own officers, as the first units in the Confederate army had done.

Some armies developed great affection for their generals. General George B. McClellan, the short figure facing President Lincoln, was beloved by his troops.

Later, the Confederate government took further steps to add soldiers. On February 17, 1864, it passed a law requiring veterans to re-enlist. In reality, by then, most of them had already done so. In the end, a high percentage of Southerners signed up to fight. The exact numbers are unknown, but one study concluded that out of about 1 million available Southern men, as many as 750,000 served.

Northern Steps

The North also faced a manpower crisis in 1863. When the enlistment terms of about 130 regiments were due to expire, it also turned to a draft. The North's draft called for each congressional district to supply a certain number of soldiers. If the quota was not met through volunteers, men chosen randomly from the district would be drafted. Individuals could escape if they hired a substitute, paid a fee, claimed hardship, or were disabled. These exemptions raised as much opposition in the North as the exemption for holding twenty slaves did in the South.

To encourage volunteering, Congress offered a $300 bounty to men who volunteered or reenlisted. This led to a new abuse—bounty jumping. Some men enlisted, collected the bounty, and then left the army to reenlist under a new name.

In 1864, the Union faced another crisis when its core of veterans who

Unrest over the draft combined with economic insecurity and racism produced a violent explosion in New York City. Horatio Seymour, the Democratic governor, spoke fiercely against the draft. At the same time, a large number of poor people, including many Irish immigrants, worried that freed African Americans would compete with them for jobs. When Union army officials came to the city in mid-July 1863 to draft New Yorkers, a riot broke out. Over several days, rioters

New York City's draft riots were the worst outbreak of civil unrest during the war.

burned buildings, beat or killed some African Americans, battled police, and chanted slogans such as "Down with the rich!" The government needed to bring troops into the city to restore order, but more than one hundred people were killed. Nearly 10 percent were African American, but the great majority were the rioters killed by the soldiers. The high number of deaths makes it the worst riot in American history.

had enlisted in 1861 was nearing the end of their three-year terms. A new law gave those who reenlisted a $400 bounty plus a thirty-day furlough, or leave of absence. In addition, the law allowed a regiment to keep its original identity if 75 percent of the veterans agreed to reenlist. In the end, nearly 60 percent of these veterans did reenlist.

These measures gave the Union most of the men it needed. By the end of the Civil War in 1865, about 2 million whites and another 200,000 African Americans fought for the Union. Tens of thousands more African Americans escaped slavery and helped Union forces as cooks, laborers, and other helpers.

Desertions

Both sides were plagued by **desertions**. Some of these escaping soldiers had been physically injured or

Winslow Homer's painting *Prisoners from the Front* highlights the contrasting fortunes of the Union and Confederate armies. Note the shabby uniforms of the Southerners and the crisp, well-dressed Northerners; as the war continued, the Confederates struggled to arm and clothe themselves adequately.

emotionally scarred by battle. Many, especially in the South, deserted because they wanted to care for their families, many of whom were struggling to get by.

This problem of desertions for the Confederate army reached major proportions in the winter of 1864 to 1865. In just one month, nearly 10 percent of the troops—about five thousand men—went home. By this time, Confederate soldiers had few clothes, little food, and dwindling stores of ammunition. Many wished to help their families—some because their families now lived in areas under Union control, and they feared what might

"There is already a heap of men gone home, and a heap [more] says if their famil[ie]s get to suffering that they will go."

Mississippi private, 1862

happen to them. Many simply believed that the war was over.

The Union had deserters, too, perhaps as many as 200,000. Rates rose following difficult battles. After the Confederates thrashed Union troops at Fredericksburg, Virginia, in December 1862, for instance, the Union army lost as many as a hundred soldiers every day. Desertion could be punishable by death, but that penalty was applied only about 140 times, far less often than the actual number of desertions.

*"Shocking and solemn as such scenes were, I do not believe that the shooting of a deserter had any great deterring influence on the **rank and file;** for the opportunities to get away safely were most abundant."*

Former Union soldier
John Billings, 1888

was that many men knew their officers well, having grown up with them since childhood.

Typically, soldiers elected the lieutenants and captains that led the companies. Regimental officers—colonels and majors—were chosen by the soldiers, by company officers, or by state governors. These officers were usually community leaders, and some had helped form their units. In some cases, wealthy men paid to provide weapons and equip the soldiers they had gathered.

The officers' corps in the South, at least at first, was stronger than in the North. Many Confederate officers had been to military school, giving them some knowledge and experience of military affairs. In the North, the vast majority of officers were completely inexperienced. Over time, though, Northern armies ended the practice of electing officers and appointed them based on their demonstrated ability.

Soldiers and Officers

Most of the soldiers of the Union and Confederate armies had been civilians, and it took a while for them to become accustomed to the discipline of military life. After the war, Confederate Carlton McCarthy recalled that "it took years to teach the educated privates in the army that it was their duty to give unquestioning obedience to officers." One reason

CHAPTER TWO

Fighting for Freedom

~

This recruiting poster, titled "Come and Join Us Brothers," aimed to bringing African Americans into the army.

The Debate over African-American Soldiers

As soon as the war broke out, many African Americans in Northern cities volunteered to fight, but the government turned them down. At the time, Lincoln worried that accepting black soldiers would push the Border States into the Confederacy.

As the war continued, however, more Northerners began to support the idea of accepting black soldiers. An 1862 law allowed freedmen—former slaves—to be organized into fighting units. A regiment was raised along the South Carolina coast in an area that the Union had seized. When these troops performed well in combat, their commander wrote glowing reports that were printed in Northern papers, encouraging the use of more African-American troops. On September 22, 1862, Lincoln declared that as of January 1, 1863, all slaves in the

Confederacy would be considered free. This Emancipation Proclamation also launched a determined effort to recruit black soldiers.

Forming Units

Starting in 1863, many new Union regiments were formed in the occupied South. Soon, units of free Northern blacks began to form in the North as well. The first were the Fifty-fourth and Fifty-fifth Massachusetts, organized by John Andrew, the antislavery governor of that state. As in all black regiments, all the officers were white; many were chosen from the state's leading families.

African-American children joined the cause, like this drummer boy.

African-American leaders urged fellow blacks to join these units. After New Orleans was captured by Union forces, a black-owned New Orleans newspaper told African Americans, "It is our duty. The nation counts on the devotion and the courage of its sons."

A Good Show

Though Northerners grew to accept the idea of black soldiers, many

GARLAND WHITE

Garland White was born into slavery in Virginia in 1829. Though it was illegal to educate a slave, he learned to read and write. At twelve, he was sold away from his family to become the personal servant of a prominent Georgia politician. Around 1860 or so, White ran away to Canada.

During the Civil War, he came to the North to help recruit African Americans to serve in the army. In late 1863, he enlisted in a black Indiana regiment, serving as the regiment's **chaplain** *and sending war news to a newspaper.*

In 1865, White's regiment was one of those that marched into Richmond, Virginia. There, in the crowd, he found his mother, whom he had not seen in more than twenty years.

wondered how they would perform. Three battles in the middle of 1863 removed any doubts. At Port Hudson, Louisiana, on May 26, two regiments of black troops charged bravely into **artillery** fire. Less than two weeks later, two other regiments beat back a fierce Confederate attack at Milliken's Bend, Louisiana. The Confederate commander acknowledged the black soldiers' bravery in his report—while pointing out that the white Union troops had run from the battle.

In 1897, Boston unveiled this monument dedicated to the Fifty-fourth Massachusetts. Engraved on the back are the names of sixty-four men from this unit who died in the assault on Fort Wagner.

The most famous of these three battles was the July 18 assault on Fort Wagner, South Carolina, by the Fifty-fourth Massachusetts. Though the unit faced withering fire from defenders, it managed to reach the fort's walls. When other regiments failed to support it sufficiently, it had to withdraw. The regiment suffered more than 250 casualties.

> *"Not a man flinched, though it was a trying time. Men fell all around me. A shell would explode and clear a space of twenty feet, [but] our men would close up [ranks] again."*
>
> Union soldier Lewis Douglass on Fort Wagner, 1863

Fort Pillow

African-American soldiers fought in many battles late in the war, most notably Fort Pillow, in Tennessee. The fort was held by nearly six hundred Union troops, almost half of them black. In April 1864, Major General Nathan Bedford Forrest's Confederate raiders attacked. After fierce fighting, the Union soldiers surrendered. Nearly two-thirds of all the black troops in the fort were killed, many after they had surrendered.

The incident did not surprise black soldiers. The sight of African-American troops enraged many

Nearly two-thirds of the black soldiers at Fort Pillow were killed, some at point-blank range as shown in this print. There is no evidence of the civilian deaths depicted in this print, however.

Confederates, who were fighting to maintain slavery. An 1862 Confederate order said that officers of black troops should be executed. Later that year, President Davis said that captured black soldiers should be turned over to state governments, which could place them back in slavery. The Fort Pillow massacre did not deter other black soldiers, though; it only made them determined to fight hard so they did not suffer the same fate.

"The delight of the colored population, in welcoming our troops, can neither be expressed nor described. Old men and women, tottering on their canes, would make their way to a Union soldier . . . and exclaim, 'Thank God . . . that I have lived to see this day!'"

Sergeant John Brock, on his unit's entry into Richmond, 1865

Perhaps the most satisfying service performed by the African-American troops came toward the end of the war. Black soldiers were the first Union troops to enter both Charleston, South Carolina, and Richmond, Virginia. The soldiers from these units undoubtedly felt a powerful mixture of pride and satisfaction as they marched through Charleston, the city where secession had been born and Richmond, the capital of the Confederacy.

The Treatment of Black Troops

The African-American troops suffered some discrimination. Many units were assigned chiefly to heavy labor such as digging trenches or moving heavy equipment, which annoyed the soldiers, who wanted to fight. The army issued a rule ending this practice, but not all commanders followed the new rule.

In addition, black soldiers were paid less than whites. In protest, the two Massachusetts units refused to accept any pay. As a result, the families of many soldiers suffered while Congress debated an equal-pay bill, which it finally passed in June 1864.

Many black soldiers also protested the fact that all the officers were white. The policy was eased, but only slightly; by the war's end, only about a hundred African Americans had been named as officers.

Distinguished Service

Several African-American soldiers distinguished themselves with exceptional bravery. During the fight at Fort Wagner, Sergeant William H. Carney of the Fifty-fourth Massachusetts picked up a fallen U.S. flag and tried to rally the troops by waving it from on top of the fort's walls. Though severely wounded in the hip, Carney held his ground until the unit's retreat. Much later, he was given the Congressional Medal of Honor, the first African American to be so honored. Sergeant Carney was not alone, however. Twenty other black fighting men also won this award.

William Carney received his Medal of Honor in 1900, about the time this photograph was taken.

A CONFEDERATE DEBATE

Late in the war, the Confederate government began thinking about bringing African Americans into its armies to help meet manpower needs. The issue was hotly debated. By February 1865, Jefferson Davis thought the South had to turn slaves into soldiers, but many disagreed. In early 1865, the backing of General Robert E. Lee and the collapsing war effort tipped the scales. The Confederate Congress narrowly passed a law allowing the government to arm slaves, but it did not approve freeing those who fought.

Uniforms and Weapons

CHAPTER THREE

Both armies used different uniforms for different branches of service.
The cavalryman fourth from left in the top row has a shorter coat than
the infantrymen to the left. Notice the different rank insignia as well.

The Soldiers' Uniforms

The Civil War is thought of as a battle between Union soldiers in blue and
Confederate troops in gray. Early in the war, however, uniforms were not standardized, causing deadly mix-ups. At several battles, Union troops did not fire
upon gray- or blue-clad Confederates, believing them to be from the North. They
paid for this error with many casualties.

In response, the Union standardized its uniforms. Soldiers wore light blue pants and a darker blue tunic. At first, manufacturers used poor-quality material that was called "shoddy." The word "shoddy" came to mean something poorly made. Over time, the Union's War Department made sure that uniforms were of better quality.

The Confederacy settled on gray jackets and blue trousers as its regulation uniform, but there were not enough Southern factories to make these. Many soldiers had to ask their families to provide homemade clothes, which were typically dyed a brownish color called butternut.

Most Union enlisted men wore a kepi, a short, circular hat with a flat top and a short visor. Officers and cavalrymen wore hats with broad brims.

Many Southern soldiers wore broad-brimmed hats as well.

Infantry Weapons

When the war began, many soldiers used old-fashioned, **smoothbore** muskets that loaded at the muzzle, or opening, at the end of the barrel. Both armies moved to give their soldiers a more advanced weapon, **rifled** muskets. The grooves cut into the inside of their barrels made them more accurate at a

The North's cavalrymen, or soldiers mounted on horses, were equipped with revolvers like this one.

greater range. For both types of guns, a cartridge holding the powder and ball inside a paper wrapper had to be reloaded and tamped down before every shot. Still, it was possible to load and shoot as many as three rounds in a minute, which was more quickly than in the past.

The war also produced a newer weapon, the breech-loading gun. Soldiers using these guns loaded bullets into the side, or the breech. Mainly used by Union armies, some of these weapons were repeating guns, allowing soldiers to fire many shots in rapid succession without reloading. Confederates angrily called this the gun that could be "loaded on Sunday and fired all week." Still, these guns were only in the hands of a minority of soldiers; rifled muskets were generally the rule.

Artillery

Cannons fired by artillery units supported the infantry. The two most popular cannons were the brass, smoothbore Napoleon and the smaller, cast-iron, rifled Parrot. The Parrot, because it was rifled, had longer range and was effective against opposing artillery. Gunners were wary of it, however, because it often exploded in heavy use. Though the smoothbore's range was shorter, this weapon worked well against an infantry attack.

IDENTIFYING SOLDIERS

Soldiers today wear name tags for easy identification if they are killed in action. Soldiers in the Civil War had nothing like this. Some could be identified by fellow soldiers or from personal effects they carried such as letters from home or books. As the war dragged on, many soldiers began to pin slips of paper with their names written on them on their chests before they went into battle. Spotting a chance to make money, a New York company sold soldiers specially printed badges with their names and addresses.

Seven soldiers were needed to arm and fire each gun as quickly as twice a minute. The cannon fired shells—hollow spheres containing an explosive charge—to attack distant targets. For closer targets, such as charging infantry, they used canisters—tin cans filled with lead balls that would scatter when exploded—harming a number of attackers at once.

Six guns were joined together in a Union **battery**, but there were only four in a Confederate battery. One problem that plagued the South was that it had a variety of guns, even in the same battery, which made it difficult to supply them.

The Union cannons shown here were the heavy artillery used to batter down the enemy's fortifications.

Meeting the Need for Weapons

The North had roughly five times the number of factories as the South did when the war began. These factories churned out the guns, cannons, and ammunition needed to equip the Union armies.

For guns, the Confederacy mostly used rifles it bought overseas and weapons it captured from the Union. The South did establish some arms factories, however. One, which made rifles, used machinery stolen from the North. The Confederacy also benefited from the excellent work of Josiah Gorgas, the official in charge of supplying the army with weapons and ammunition.

The dozens of cannon balls in the foreground and the many cannons lined up behind show the power of Union factories.

Battle Tactics

The new weapons gave great power to defenders. Rifled muskets and cannons could hit targets more accurately and do more damage from farther away. Defenders increased their advantage by digging trenches and building **breastworks** to hide behind, making themselves harder to hit. At the same time, attacking artillery could no longer move forward with attacking infantry to get close to the defenders' lines, as it had in earlier wars. Since the defending infantry had longer-range guns than before, these soldiers could pick off the people manning the cannons, weakening the attackers' force. Because infantry could load their guns using cartridges, defenders could also fire more quickly—as much as three times in a minute.

As a result of these changes in weaponry, attacking forces were at a major disadvantage. Indeed, attackers had to outnumber a defensive force by three to one to have a chance to defeat dug-in troops. Yet generals continued to favor older tactics that were based on direct assaults by large bodies of troops. In some battles, these attacks worked. In most cases, though, they failed completely since oncoming troops became easy targets. Frontal attacks typically led to high casualties among the attackers.

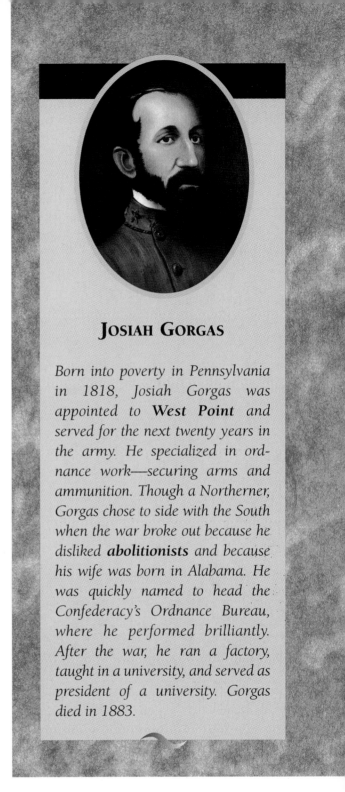

JOSIAH GORGAS

Born into poverty in Pennsylvania in 1818, Josiah Gorgas was appointed to **West Point** *and served for the next twenty years in the army. He specialized in ordnance work—securing arms and ammunition. Though a Northerner, Gorgas chose to side with the South when the war broke out because he disliked* **abolitionists** *and because his wife was born in Alabama. He was quickly named to head the Confederacy's Ordnance Bureau, where he performed brilliantly. After the war, he ran a factory, taught in a university, and served as president of a university. Gorgas died in 1883.*

Other aspects of Civil War battles made attacks difficult. Commanders often planned coordinated attacks in which two wings hit the enemy in two places at the same time. This prevented the enemy commanders from moving troops from a quiet part of the battlefield to an area of fierce fighting. The commanders, however, were then leading tens of thousands of soldiers spread out over many miles, and communication between different groups was difficult without radios or

"It was thought to be a great thing to charge a battery of artillery or an earthwork lined with infantry. . . . We were very lavish of blood in those days."

Confederate D. H. Hill, commenting on Civil War tactics, 1888

telephones. Delays between the sending and the receiving of messages made it difficult to actually coordinate attacks.

Moving the Troops

The North developed a powerful industrial-age army. Teams of engineers built or repaired tracks so trains could carry supplies and soldiers wherever needed and quickly put up

Engineers built bridges to carry trains over creeks and valleys. Often these bridges were destroyed when enemy cavalry troops raided behind the army's lines.

These Union soldiers are carrying out marching drills in camp. When armies of tens of thousands of soldiers were on the move, the march covered many miles.

bridges, often **pontoon bridges**, to allow troops to cross rivers. One observer said with amazement, "The Yankees [Northerners] can build bridges quicker than the Rebs [Southerners] can burn them down." The South also used trains to speed supplies and soldiers to battlefields.

While railroads were important, most armies moved the traditional way—on their feet. In hot, dry summers, marching soldiers were choked with dust. In heavy rain, the dirt roads they traveled turned to mud, slowing an army's advance.

THE STONEWALL BRIGADE

Infantry in the Civil War typically marched about 2.5 miles (4 kilometers) an hour. Confederate general Thomas J. "Stonewall" Jackson's troops won fame as "foot cavalry" because they could cover up to 6 miles (10 km) an hour—more than double the speed of the normal march.

CHAPTER FOUR

Camp Life

"It is monotonous, it is not monotonous, it is laborious, it is lazy, it is a bore, it is a lark, it is half war, half peace, and totally attractive, and not to be dispensed with from one's experience in the nineteenth century."

Union private Theodore Winthrop on camp life, 1861

~

Army Camps

The armies did not spend all their time in battle or on the march. Much of the war—perhaps most of it—was spent in camp.

Union tents slept two soldiers who spread blankets on the ground for a bed. For winter quarters, they built wooden shelters to better protect them from the cold. Confederates used similar tents. Over time, though, the lack of supplies forced Southern soldiers to make do with less. Many simply spread a piece of waterproof oilcloth on the ground and covered themselves with a blanket. If it was raining, they put another piece of oilcloth on top of the blanket. Officers in both armies had tents that were larger than the two-person tents.

Because many people were crowded into a relatively small area, camps were generally not healthy places. Little was known at that time about the connection between sanitation and disease. Tens of thousands of soldiers became ill, and many of them died. Some diseases were caused by poor food or unsanitary conditions. Some men were felled by infectious diseases, such as measles, that were passed to people who had never been exposed to them.

This camp shows several different styles of tent that were in use during the Civil War. In the foreground, Confederate prisoners sit on the grass.

Routine Life

The day began at five or six in the morning with roll call, followed by any special orders of the day. After breakfast came sick call, when those who were ill reported to the medical staff. Many did not report, sharing the view of an Alabama private that "the doctors kill more than they cure." Then came fatigue duty, or cleaning up the camp. Next came **drills**, followed by lunch and more drills. Late in the day, the soldiers assembled to hear any general orders from the army's commander. As one soldier noted, this was also the time that they heard "lectures on the

These soldiers use a makeshift scale to weigh out their **rations** of food for a meal.

shortcomings of the company." The soldiers then had dinner and some time to relax until 8:30 p.m., when

Sundays, which included religious services, provided a break from the mind-numbing routine of camp life.

they assembled again for the day's final roll call. Soldiers were to be in bed and quiet a half an hour later.

Camp life could be very boring. One Union private explained that mornings were spent in "drill, then drill, then drill again," adding that "Between drills, we drill and sometimes we stop to eat a little."

Supplying the Troops

The Union built up huge supply depots that held tons of food, uniforms, and ammunition. An army of 100,000 on the move needed 600 tons (550 metric tons) of supplies every day. The North used steamboats and trains to haul these goods long distances. When troops were out of reach of railroads, long supply lines of wagons trailed behind them.

Confederate forces traveled much lighter. First, they were closer to their sources of supply. Second, they were forced to—the branch of the army charged with providing supplies failed badly. One problem was the lack of railroads, which made it difficult to move supplies. As a result, food sometimes never got out of warehouses, where it simply spoiled. (Sometimes mismanagement caused the same problem for the Union armies.) Many Confederate soldiers enjoyed better food when they took over a Union camp.

In a few campaigns, armies abandoned their supply lines, and advancing soldiers simply took food from the land they passed through. Union general Sherman's famous march through Georgia in 1864 is the most notable example. Sometimes, however, this "foraging" fell into nothing more than looting as soldiers grabbed families'

"We can't get vegetables of any description. Our rations are one pound of [corn] meal and one fourth pound of bacon a day. . . . I just believe that I could eat as much more as I get and then not have enough."

William Leak, Confederate private, 1864

household goods and stole farm animals.

The Lighter Side

Soldiers in camp did have some time to themselves. They entertained themselves by playing cards, telling stories, and singing songs. They read mail from home and wrote letters to their families. These letters helped them feel more connected to life on the home front. If camped near a city in a period of relative quiet, they might receive a pass allowing them an evening's entertainment. They also played a newly popular sport—baseball.

Even though they were prisoners of war, these Union soldiers had the chance to enjoy an occasional game of baseball.

WOMEN SOLDIERS

Some women actually served as soldiers, though they had to disguise themselves as men to do so. Some were discovered and dismissed, but some, like Frances Clayton of Minnesota and Amy Clarke of Mississippi, simply enlisted again. Some women soldiers stayed disguised during their entire term of enlistment. Jennie Hodgers served in an Illinois regiment as Albert Cashier for three years before being honorably discharged in 1865. One fellow soldier said, "I never suspected at any time . . . that Cashier was a woman."

This photograph captures a restful scene at a Union army camp featuring three women and two young children. An older boy stands proudly to the right next to the flag. The women appear uncomfortable with being photographed—none of the three is looking at the camera.

Sometimes there was contact between the two sides when opposing armies camped near each other. Southern soldiers often had extra tobacco, and Northerners had more coffee and sugar. In times of quiet, the two sides sometimes traded these luxuries or swapped newspapers.

"Daughters of the Regiment"

As in many wars, some women came along with the armies. Some joined as "daughters of the regiment," women who cooked, repaired uniforms, or washed clothes for the soldiers. They often helped care for the wounded when a battle took place, and some showed as much bravery under fire as the soldiers did.

Annie Etheridge, who served for the Union, was one of the most famous of these women. Etheridge was given a horse and hired to cook for the corps' officers but spent most of her time with her regiment. Another example was Susie Baker, an escaped slave who joined one of the regiments of African-American soldiers. She eventually married one of the sergeants in the unit.

> "No march was too long or weather too inclement to deter this patriotic woman from doing what she considered her duty."

Confederate private on Lucy Ann Cox, who served as a nurse with the Thirteenth Virginia

ANNIE ETHERIDGE

Born in Detroit in 1840, Annie Etheridge married James Etheridge in 1860 and went into the army with him when he enlisted. Though her husband deserted, Etheridge remained with the army until the end of the war.

Although she did not fight, Etheridge was at most of the major battles in the East, from First Bull Run in 1861 to the war's end. When the fighting started, she came onto the battlefield to care for troops. One soldier wrote, "The balls fall thick and fast around her, but she fears them not, and [cares for the wounded] as if she was in camp and out of danger."

After the war, Etheridge worked for a time as a clerk in a government office. After she died in 1913, she was buried in Arlington National Cemetery in Virginia, a distinct honor.

CHAPTER FIVE

Medical Care

*"A wound from a smooth-
bore and a round shot striking the
thigh bone was often deflected with no
serious injury to the bone. . . . A minié ball
fired from a grooved [rifled] musket under
similar conditions might not only fracture,
but crush two or three inches of the bone."*

A. G. Hart, Civil War surgeon, 1902

~

The Wounded and the Sick

The new rifled guns could fire more accurately and from longer range. This—plus the tactic of massed assaults against well-protected defenders—led to heavy casualties. A major problem for the medical staff was the bullet used in the war, the minié ball. It often shattered the bone when it hit, causing many soldiers to lose an arm or a leg. Adding to the problem of wounds was the spread of disease.

Problems with Medical Care

Civil War doctors faced enormous challenges with few tools to use against them. They had no way to replace lost blood and no antibiotics to fight disease or infection. Indeed, no one understood that germs cause disease or that operating rooms and instruments must be kept clean to prevent infections. Surgeons had some drugs for anesthesia, which made patients unconscious during the surgery, but these medicines were not always available, especially in the South. Many patients, thus, faced surgery wide-awake.

Assistant surgeons treated the wounded behind the lines, bandaging minor wounds and sending those with major problems to surgeons in field hospitals away from the fighting. These hospitals were typically set up in people's homes, taken by the army for temporary use. Many amputations were performed in field

This image of a field hospital shows how crude conditions were. Wounded soldiers often lingered outside in unsanitary crowds after treatment.

DAN SICKLES'S LEG

Some of the wounded showed a grim sense of humor. Dan Sickles, a Union general, had his leg smashed by a cannonball while commanding his troops at the battle in Gettysburg, Pennsylvania, in July 1863. As frequently happened with such wounds, Sickles's lower leg was amputated. He directed the doctors to send the bone to the Army Medical Museum in Washington, D.C. After the war, Sickles visited his former limb from time to time.

Dan Sickles (left), shown with a fellow general, lost his right leg at Gettysburg.

CLARA BARTON

Born in 1821 in Massachusetts, Clara Barton was taught at home. By the time she was fifteen, she had spent two years nursing a sick brother and was starting a career as a teacher. At thirty, she headed a school in Bordentown, New Jersey. The school grew so large the town did not believe a woman could run it. When a male principal was named in her place, Barton quit.

After the First Battle of Bull Run in 1861, Barton began nursing wounded soldiers and searching for the missing. She spent the rest of the war in this work, earning the nickname "Angel of the Battlefield."

After the war, Barton heard about the recently formed International Committee of the Red Cross in Europe, which cared for wounded soldiers. She then organized the American Red Cross, which also helped people suffering from natural disasters. She died in 1912.

hospitals—in dirty rooms on dirty tables with dirty instruments that were used over and over again. Soldiers were then bandaged up as well as possible. Those who needed further care were sent back to military hospitals.

Improvements in Medical Care

Some reformers formed the U.S. Sanitary Commission and similar groups to fix such medical problems. They investigated and reported on problems in field hospitals and got Congress to pass laws to improve conditions. They also raised money to buy bandages, medicines, and other supplies. Most importantly, the Sanitary Commission set up hospital ships and hospitals in Northern cities where the wounded could receive better care.

In medical care, as in many of the support services, the Confederacy lagged behind the Union. It lacked the doctors and medicines needed to care for the wounded and an organized effort to improve health care comparable to the Sanitary Commission. On the other hand, Chimborazo Hospital in Richmond, Virginia, was the largest military hospital in the world and could handle about forty-five hundred patients at a time.

The dedicated Civil War doctors also deserve some credit. They faced difficult circumstances with few

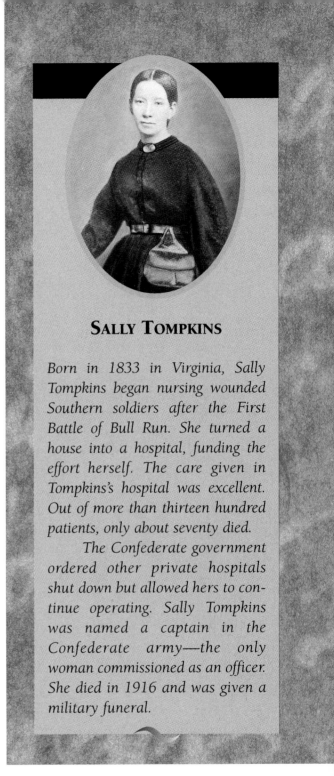

SALLY TOMPKINS

Born in 1833 in Virginia, Sally Tompkins began nursing wounded Southern soldiers after the First Battle of Bull Run. She turned a house into a hospital, funding the effort herself. The care given in Tompkins's hospital was excellent. Out of more than thirteen hundred patients, only about seventy died.

The Confederate government ordered other private hospitals shut down but allowed hers to continue operating. Sally Tompkins was named a captain in the Confederate army—the only woman commissioned as an officer. She died in 1916 and was given a military funeral.

resources at a time of limited medical knowledge. While two soldiers died of disease for every one killed in combat, this was actually an improvement over the rates in wars earlier in the 1800s.

Pioneering Women

Many of those who helped care for the wounded were women. Until the Civil War, nursing had been considered a male profession, but thousands of women volunteered to care for the wounded in both the North and South. One volunteer nurse in the South remarked, "I have never worked so hard in all my life and I would rather do that than anything else in the world."

Some nurses worked throughout the war. Others served temporarily when a battle was fought near their homes or took care of wounded family members. Some, such as Clara Barton, Sally Tompkins, and Mary Ann Bickerdyke, became well known for their work. The work of these pioneers changed attitudes about what women could do.

CHAPTER SIX

Spies and Guerrillas

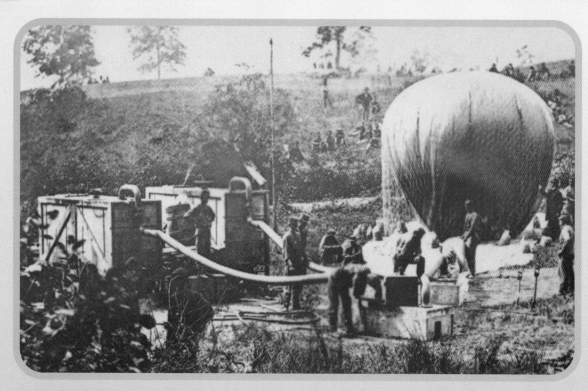

Union general George McClellan sent observers into the air in lighter-than-air balloons. From these high perches, they could see where Southern forces were placed.

Army Intelligence

Both sides used civilians to try to learn about the size and movements of enemy forces. Southern armies could count on locals to pass along information about Union armies moving through southern land. Union armies had their own resources; the stream of African Americans who escaped slavery and made their way to Northern lines often brought useful information with them. Harriet Tubman, a former slave famous for her work on the **Underground Railroad**

ROSE GREENHOW

Born in Maryland in 1817, Rose O'Neal Greenhow was a well-known hostess in Washington, D.C. Many important political and military leaders attended her parties. Devoted to the South, Greenhow sent messages to Confederate general P. G. T. Beauregard before First Bull Run in 1861 that told him when the Union army would march against him and how large the force was. Northern officials arrested her later that year, but even in prison she passed messages to Southern leaders. She was found guilty of spying in 1862 and sent to Richmond, where she was welcomed with cheers. Greenhow spent the next two years in Europe. On her return to the South in 1864, her ship was approached by a Union cruiser. Fearing capture, Greenhow escaped in a small boat, which capsized in rough seas. She drowned, weighed down by her heavy skirts, her coat, and the gold coins she was trying to bring to the Confederacy.

and in the abolitionist movement before the war, set up a network of blacks in the Carolinas who fed information to the Union army.

In Virginia, the Union army tried to organize the effort of gathering accurate intelligence. General George McClellan hired detective Allan Pinkerton in mid-1861 to head his information-gathering operation.

Pinkerton and his agents did a good job of tracking down Confederate spies, but his reports overestimated the size of the Confederate army.

Some of the intelligence gatherers became famous spies, and several of the most colorful were women. The Confederacy had Belle Boyd, who passed useful information to General "Stonewall" Jackson and was arrested, and Rose Greenhow. The Union had Elizabeth Van Lew, who used African Americans to pass information from her home in Richmond. Actress Pauline Cushman delivered useful intelligence about Confederate troops in Tennessee. When captured, Cushman was sentenced to be executed but was left behind when the Confederate army retreated.

Guerrilla Fighters

To win the war, the Union had to defeat Confederate armies and invade the South, which meant that it had to hold large areas of Southern territory in the face of a hostile population. As a result, the Northern army often had to face guerrillas. These fighters were not part of a regular army and were able to strike quickly, by surprise, and then escape.

There were several areas in which guerrilla activity aimed at both civilians and Union soldiers. Among the most prominent areas were Missouri, Tennessee, and the Shenandoah Valley of Virginia. Each held Unionists, or pro-Northern people. However, Confederate supporters made life difficult for these people, harassing and sometimes even killing them. Union soldiers often came into these areas trying to catch the guerrillas, but the Southerners were too quick and escaped.

The most famous guerrilla leaders were Missouri's William Quantrill and Virginia's John Mosby. Quantrill had had run-ins with the law before the war began. He first joined the Confederate army but soon left it to form a guerrilla band. To the North, these men were outlaws. To the South, they were rangers—romantic heroes, not outlaws.

Quantrill's band of nearly 500 included many men, such as Cole and Jim Younger and Jesse and Frank James, who later became outlaws of the West. In 1863, Quantrill led his force into Lawrence, Kansas, where it killed 150 men and destroyed about $500,000 in property. Nearly two months later, his force dressed in Union uniforms and surprised a troop of real Northern soldiers, killing nearly one hundred. Quantrill died in an 1865 raid.

Mosby controlled his area so completely that parts of northern Virginia were called "Mosby's

His rangers captured Union supply wagons and destroyed telegraph lines. Despite many efforts, Northern forces could never stop Mosby's raiders. Soon after Robert E. Lee surrendered, Mosby disbanded his outfit.

Union forces struck back after Confederate guerrilla attacks, often levying fines on the people in an area to pay for the damage done to Union supplies and troops. They also arrested important people in the towns nearby, hoping the citizens would put pressure on the guerrillas to stop. Sometimes Union soldiers burned houses and seized or destroyed people's property. These actions often embittered pro-Confederacy people even more.

John Mosby's most famous exploit was the capture of a Union general who was in bed just 10 miles (16 km) from Washington, D.C.

"All day long the soldiers continue to destroy property. . . . Many hundreds of sheep, cattle and hogs and . . . poultry are destroyed. . . . One half of this truly unfortunate country have been robbed to destitution and the other half have nothing to spare for their relief."

Unknown witness to Union response to guerrilla attacks

Confederacy." Mosby's force numbered in the hundreds, though it was usually broken up into small units.

CHAPTER SEVEN

Prisoners of War

~

Hundreds of Confederate prisoners stand outside their barracks at the Union's Camp Douglas, near Chicago.

Taking Prisoners

Beginning in the first battle of the war, both sides captured enemy soldiers who had surrendered. The rules of war called for these soldiers to be treated humanely, and, at first, both sides tried to meet those standards. Of course, the Confederacy could not afford to lose soldiers and asked to exchange prisoners. The Union hesitated, concerned that such an agreement gave some form of recognition to the Confederates.

After western victories early in 1862, however, the Union suddenly had thousands of prisoners and few facilities for them. In the summer of 1862, the

Confederacy and the Union sides agreed to exchange prisoners. If one side held more than the other, the extra men would be released. However, those men had to promise to stay out of combat until an equal number of men were released from the other side. This arrangement was called paroling.

Prisoner exchanges continued for nearly a year, but two problems arose. First, the South threatened to execute captured African-American soldiers. In response, the U.S. Congress stopped the exchanges. Second, when Union general Ulysses S. Grant took Vicksburg, Mississippi, in July 1863, he suddenly had 30,000 Confederate soldiers as prisoners. Unwilling to hold so many prisoners, Grant released them on parole. The Confederacy, claiming legal problems with the parole, put them back in uniform, angering Union officials who thought the act was dishonest. The Union then stopped all exchanges.

A Harsh Life

The end of exchanges caused a catastrophe. As prisons filled, conditions became awful, especially in the South. There, dwindling supplies made it difficult to feed the army and the civilian population, let alone prisoners. Often makeshift, the prison

THE TREATMENT OF BLACK PRISONERS

While Southerners said they would kill African-American prisoners, they did not always carry out that threat. There were certainly cases, such as at Fort Pillow in Tennessee in April 1864, of Southern troops killing black soldiers who had surrendered. There were also threats to send black soldiers into slavery. This does not seem to have been done, however. Still, African-American prisoners—and their white officers— often received harsher treatment than other prisoners.

facilities were inadequate. Southern officials, after all, expected that exchanges would be renewed at some point, and they did not prepare better facilities.

The worst conditions in the South were at the Andersonville prison camp in Georgia. The prison was horribly overcrowded. Prisoners suffered from starvation, disease, filth, bad water, and exposure to the hot sun and the cold winter. Three thousand died in August 1864 alone. The final death toll for the prison reached over 12,000.

Andersonville, in Georgia, was the most notorious Southern prison during the war. Built to hold ten thousand men, it eventually imprisoned more than three times that number.

Some Northerners believed the Confederates deliberately aimed to punish Union prisoners. The Union retaliated by cutting the amount of food it gave to Confederate prisoners.

Many of these prisoners were already suffering, however, since some Northern prisons were just as bad as Southern ones. At a prison camp in New York, nearly 10 percent of the eighty-four hundred prisoners died in a three-month span, typically from malnutrition and disease. The situation in Northern prisons worsened in late 1864 as more and more Southern prisoners entered the system.

At the same time, pressure mounted in the North to resume exchanges. Abraham Lincoln refused to budge, however, as long as the Southerners would not agree to

Henry Wirz, the Confederate commander at Andersonville, was hanged for his treatment of Northern prisoners. Historians still debate whether the trial was fair since Wirz seems more a victim of Northern anger over the treatment of prisoners than a war criminal. He was the only person executed for war crimes in the Civil War.

exchange black soldiers the same as white ones. The Confederacy did not accept this.

The Toll

Because conditions were so poor, thousands of prisoners on both sides died. Official records put deaths of Union prisoners in Confederate facilities at more than 30,000, about 15 percent of all Union soldiers held in Southern prisons. Nearly 26,000 Southern prisoners died in the Union facilities, approximately 12 percent of the total number of Confederate prisoners. The estimate of Union deaths is probably too low, however. At the infamous Andersonville prison in Georgia, nearly one-third of the prisoners died.

"The allowance to each man has been one small loaf of bread (it takes three to make a pound) and a piece of meat, two inches square, per day.... Lately [this ration] has been reduced.... Such is the wretched, ravenous condition of these poor starving creatures that ... they are trapping rats and mice for food. . . . Many of them are nearly naked, barefooted, bareheaded, and without bed-clothes; exposed to ceaseless torture from the chill."

Article in the *New York Daily News* on Confederate soldiers in an Illinois prison, 1865

Time Line

1861 *Mar. 6:* Confederate Congress calls for 100,000 troops.
Apr. 12: South fires on Fort Sumter, beginning Civil War.
June 8: Union sets up U.S. Sanitary Commission to look into medical conditions.

1862 *Apr. 16:* President Jefferson Davis signs first Confederate draft law.
July 17: U.S. Congress authorizes recruiting African Americans into the army.
July 22: Union and Confederacy agree to exchange prisoners.

1863 *Feb. 25:* U.S. Congress passes draft law.
May 13: Fifty-fourth Massachusetts, first black regiment, officially mustered into service.
May 26: African-American troops fight bravely at Port Hudson, Louisiana.

June 7: Black troops fight well at Milliken's Bend, Louisiana.
July 12–17: Riots ignite in New York City over draft law, killing more than one hundred people.
July 18: Fifty-fourth Massachusetts fights at Fort Wagner, South Carolina.
Aug. 21: Confederate William Quantrill raids Lawrence, Kansas.
Oct. 6: Quantrill massacres ninety Union soldiers at Baxter Springs, Kansas.

1864 *Feb. 17:* Confederate law requires veterans to reenlist.
Apr. 12: Black soldiers at Fort Pillow, Tennessee, are massacred.
June 15: U.S. Congress grants equal pay to African-American soldiers.

1865 *Mar. 13:* Confederate law allows slaves to join army.

Glossary

abolitionist: someone who believes in abolishing, or ending, slavery.

artillery: large, heavy weapons such as cannons; also used to refer to the branch of the army that uses such weapons.

battery: an artillery unit in the army.

Border States: the states on the northern edge of the southern states, where there was slavery, but it was not a very strong part of society; includes Delaware, Maryland, Kentucky, and Missouri.

breastworks: defenses made of wood that soldiers could hide behind to fire on an attacking force.

casualties: the people killed, wounded, captured, and missing in a battle.

chaplain: a person who conducts religious services for part of the military, an organization, or a family.

Confederacy: also called "the South;" another name for the Confederate States of America, the nation formed by the states that had seceded, or split off from, the United States—Virginia, Tennessee, North Carolina, South Carolina, Georgia, Alabama, Mississippi, Louisiana, Texas, Arkansas, and Florida.

desertions: soldiers leaving the army before their terms of enlistment are up.

draft: a law that requires men of a certain age to join the military.

drills: exercises that train soldiers in precise marching and movement of weapons.

pontoon bridge: a series of flat-bottomed boats or floats joined together and covered with wooden planks that soldiers, animals, and wagons could travel across.

rank and file: the ordinary soldiers and sailors, not the officers.

ration: a fixed portion of food allowed to each soldier for each day.

regiment: a unit of the army that included ten companies of one hundred soldiers each.

rifled: having spiral grooves cut inside a barrel; rifling increases a gun's accuracy.

secede: to formally withdraw from an organization; in the case of the Civil War, it means to leave the Union. *Secession* is the act of seceding.

smoothbore: having a barrel with a smooth inner surface.

Underground Railroad: a secret network of people who worked together to help runaway slaves get to free states or to Canada before and during the Civil War.

Union: also called "the North;" another name for the United States of America, which, after secession, included Maine, New Hampshire, Vermont, Massachusetts, Rhode Island, Connecticut, New York, New Jersey, Pennsylvania, Delaware, Maryland, Ohio, Michigan, Indiana, Illinois, Kentucky, Wisconsin, Minnesota, Iowa, Kansas, Missouri, Oregon, and California; in 1863, West Virginia seceded from Virginia and entered the Union

West Point: the United States Military Academy located in West Point, New York.

Further Resources

These web sites and books cover the lives of soldiers and civilians, men and women, spies and doctors working throughout the Civil War:

WEB SITES

www.civilwarhome.com Follow links on this Civil War enthusiast's homepage to letters about the war to and from soldiers, biographies, and other articles.

www.homepages.dsu.edu/jankej/civil-war/civilwar.htm An index web site lists numerous articles on a wide range of Civil War topics, including army life, "colored troops," women in the war, flags, prisoners, and medicine. Also includes a way to search for specific soldiers and sailors.

sunsite.utk.edu/civil-war/warweb.html The American Civil War web site contains a number of links to resources, including images of wartime, regimental histories, and essays on music and prisoners.

www.civil-war.net The Civil War Home Page web site includes entries of soldiers' diaries and letters home and slave narratives. Also contains essays on women in the Civil War and death statistics.

BOOKS

Blashfield, Jean F. *Women at the Front: Their Changing Roles in the Civil War.* New York: Franklin Watts, 1997.

Corrick, James A. *Life Among the Soldiers and Cavalry.* San Diego, CA: Lucent Books, 2000.

Haskins, Jim. *Black, Blue & Gray: African Americans in the Civil War.* New York: Simon & Schuster, 1998.

Murphy, Jim. *The Boys' War: Confederate and Union Soldiers Talk About the Civil War.* New York: Clarion Books, 1990.

Nofi, Albert A. *Spies in the Civil War.* Philadelphia, PA: Chelsea House, 2000.

Ritchie, David, and Fred Israel. *Health and Medicine.* New York: Chelsea House, 1995.

Robertson, James I. *Tenting Tonight: The Soldier's Life.* Alexandria, VA: Time-Life Books, 1999.

Savage, Douglas. *Prison Camps in the Civil War* (Untold History of the Civil War). Philadelphia, PA: Chelsea House, 2000.

Stewart, Gail B. *Weapons of War: The Civil War* (American War Library). San Diego, CA: Lucent Books, 2000.

Trudeau, Noah Andre. *Like Men of War: Black Troops in the Civil War 1862–1865.* Edison, NJ: Castle Books, 1998.

Whitelaw, Nancy. *Clara Barton: Civil War Nurse (Historical American Biographies).* Springfield, NJ: Enslow, 1997.

Zeinert, Karen. *Those Courageous Women of the Civil War.* Brookfield, CT: Millbrook Press, 1998.

Index

Page numbers in *italics* indicate maps and diagrams.